# Ageless Rainbow

Suchismita Ghoshal
Nwankwo Chukwuma Levi

**Ukiyoto Publishing**

All global publishing rights are held by

**Ukiyoto Publishing**

Published in 2023

Content Copyright © Suchismita Ghoshal, Nwankwo Chukwuma Levi
**ISBN 9789357879712**

All rights reserved.

No part of this publication may be reproduced, transmitted, or stored in a retrieval system, in any form by any means, electronic, mechanical, photocopying, recording or otherwise, without the prior permission of the publisher.

The moral rights of the author have been asserted.

This is a work of fiction. Names, characters, businesses, places, events, locales, and incidents are either the products of the author's imagination or used in a fictitious manner. Any resemblance to actual persons, living or dead, or actual events is purely coincidental.

This book is sold subject to the condition that it shall not by way of trade or otherwise, be lent, resold, hired out or otherwise circulated, without the publisher's prior consent, in any form of binding or cover other than that in which it is published.

www.ukiyoto.com

# Synopsis

**"AGELESS RAINBOW"**, the name that puts you into the world of radiant colors and brightness, holds the exact meaning of effectiveness and devotion to the lives of the authors, respectively Suchismita Ghoshal and Nwankwo Levi. Rooting from the different parts of the world, the authors have put their efficient efforts to bring literature close to this poetic collection. From dwelling into the huge source of lifestyle, perspectives, opinions, random thoughts to ranging voices to different issues, both the authors have skilled and phenomenally executed their tasks to give their readers a sense of aesthetic literature. This collection focuses on how small things can take the shape of a beautifully expressed poem. Art truly has no shape, no boundaries, no borders; all it needs is perseverance and inner zeal to look through things in an exceptional way which ordinary people miss out. Creators of this collective anthology have collaboratively initiated to reach new heights with enthusiasm, support and delocalizations of expressions. In this materialistic world that is focused on over-normalising monetary benefits, luxurious and lucrative upgrading, and highly ambitious achievement only, this book takes you to feel how to make peace and have a life energy for a peaceful state of mind.

# Contents

| | |
|---|---|
| Poems By Nwankwo Chukwuma Levi | 1 |
| | |
| Victims | 2 |
| Widow's Plight | 4 |
| Victory | 5 |
| Tender Beauties | 6 |
| Glorious Moments | 7 |
| Candles In The Wind | 8 |
| Riddles Of The Cripple And The Blind | 9 |
| The Street Legend | 11 |
| Wrinkles Of Grace | 12 |
| The Familiar Foe In Winter | 13 |
| Bread Of Sorrow | 14 |
| Where We Belong | 15 |
| In The Wings Of Time | 16 |
| Medal Of Honor | 17 |
| Beautiful Imperfections | 18 |
| | |
| Poems By Suchismita Ghoshal | 19 |
| | |
| Eternity | 20 |
| Salvation | 21 |
| Ages | 22 |
| Love-Language | 23 |
| Dreamlines | 24 |
| Symmetry Of Love | 25 |
| Artistry | 26 |
| Nomadic Insanity | 27 |
| Freedom | 28 |
| Ice-Cream | 29 |
| Heritage | 30 |
| Inheritance | 31 |
| Glorification | 32 |
| Apocalypse | 33 |
| Traits Of A Bohemian | 34 |
| About the Authors | 35 |

# Poems By Nwankwo Chukwuma Levi

## Victims

Desolate has become
this city, the walls built
around it to keep out the
Sadness has emptied the
bottles of happiness, we
are nothing but victims
of this situation.

War is banging, hunger is knocking, but a cup of peace satisfies our souls, by the news of war. Our hearts sank, for our families we love, their souls we cherish for we will become nothing but victims of this situation.

Legacies of war and bloodshed will be left, for children of the lost will learn and write on the skulls of men and women u sent to war, no one speaks for them for nothing Is heard in the battlefield, but the sounds of triggers and whisperings of bullets. for they have become victims of this situation.

Wipe your tears oh! ye mothers for we have
Seen the bodies of your sons who fought for 'Equality', dry your sorrows oh! ye wives for we
Have seen the remains of your husbands who
Died in their struggles, for they are nothing but Victims of this situation.

All these heroes will never die in vain, the land of our ancestors will avenge their deaths, for when the dusk shall age, these tyrants shall become victims of the same situation.

## Widow's Plight

Death knocked, so brutal
It was, so careless to perch
In the ears of the beloved,
A tool was stolen from her.

Feelings incompatible, a
voyage of thousand miles
approached, a seed of plight dug.
Who will fight her foes like the mountain
Wolves?

Nowhere to hide, shame crept in, she could run but she couldn't hide, for, in the wings of time, her plight shall perch.

Winters cold roared, like a famished lion, unkind shivers ran through her spins like the dews of Harmon, the soul that promised to shelter, has gone nigh to rest for its plight has come to rule the night like never.

Voices of foes thundered like the raging storm in the cities of goblins where peace and tranquility have failed to stand, wolves in sheep's clothing clustered like the web around a forgotten city so unkempt and so ancient.

Though her soul sank so deep, and her plight hugged so big but she clung to the old rugged cross believing that her jars can never run dry for Jah got her, like the lilies in the winter valleys.

# Victory

Is this not the song we sang
After we pained through?
Is this not the only gain that
Stood after we've danced
To the beats of war, for this
Medals round my neck were
The only proof to show we
Subdued our foes and out
of it stood echoes of victory.

Valiantly our souls boiled
Upon this boundary in-between us and our foes stood hostility, for the hands that held high our flag were determination and persistence, this song of victory rose because to the bare earth the heads of our foes were smashed.

Upon the belly of this naked earth lay the uncountable skulls of our enemies, besides
Its head stood tender roses, for candles of love and remembrance for them shall we burn, they were the fuel that kept awake our fire of persistence and the lyrics that lay before our songs of victory.

Our swords and guns we shall drop, we shall live all as one, for fragrances of love has filled our nostrils and its drum our skilled men shall beat, from the east shall this sun of happiness rise, from its smiles shall the scars of the earth be healed, and this trumpet of victory shall waken the intoxicated gods of the earth.

## **Tender Beauties**

I am the joy you seek when
You are sorrowful, I am the staff that stood before Pharaoh, I am the eyes that see even tomorrow, besides your rivers of sorrow lay in your box of joy, besides the mighty throne of Pharaoh, stood In his fears, for before the lazy eyes of tomorrow lay these tender beauties waiting to be born.

If ever thy hope diminishes in the wings of despair and thy happiness the garment of depression wear, please remember the patience of the night, for in every head lies a brain, in every little today there is a mighty tomorrow, for in the box of these tender lilies are new beauties waiting to be born.

I can hear the echoes of your sadness deep down, but a beautiful smile you wear like garments of many colors if thy foes with afflictions bury thy hope, remember like the seeds before the farmer in its due grows with more strength and power than lie in a box of tender beauties.

All these pains indeed I will take to Jah, shall I become a well-fed slave all my life? No! For my cup of afflictions and sorrows has overflown, I have no assurance of where my tomorrow will stand, for it is better to become a Hungry free man for I know in me, there is a bountiful beauty waiting to be born.

## Glorious Moments

Ponder through this lane,

Think of the goods left,

Scrutinize this path of the treasury, some beams illuminate the nights of men, the beams of the glorious Moments.

There is nothing, but the beauties that remain, they have golden stars in the palm of their hands, and at the base of the glittering walls of victory lay their tools of honor for before this box of memories lay their glorious moments.

Once in our lifetime, this is the greatest tragedy to befall us, In times of misery to remember when we were happy, but one star kept our hopes alive, the stars of the glorious moments.

If these labors were forgotten, and the footprints of struggles wiped, remember the Oaths taken before the edge of the sword, that our names in the sands of time forever be written, and the tales of our

Victories will forever cling to the edges of these glorious moments.

## Candles In The Wind

I know our destinies were different like guns and roses, who knows the call I could have answered if I had taken your doses, but now it seems you lived your life like candles in the wind, for this rain came like one upon the trenches.

Your antenna stood amongst us like the tall trees in the Greenwood, our memories lay in these rainbow walls so peaceful as a baby's sigh, for we shall one day dance again like the actresses of Bollywood, but now I am so sorry you've lived your life like a candle in the wind.

You burned down for too long, when my ink was still an infant, I wish you were graced to hold on for too long, I would have written my feelings to the wind to make you feel among, but I couldn't pull my trigger, for this song has gone back to the tongue that sang them.

Your dreams lay afloat on these pools, like balloons in the hands of the little boy, who only cares for candy, but before this dusk visits, I shall write them home for they've grown so cold and old like a candle in the wind.

# Riddles Of The Cripple And The Blind

To the world we are different
Entities, but to our riddles we
are one answer, with you oh!
mutilate friend I have seen the world,
With you oh! Sightless comrade
I walked down the hallway.

This is where we use to be,
When love was the only kettle that
Boils our emotions, until gossip came
And painted it black, this was once
Our abode of fantasies, until hostility
Whispered in disguise.

Nobody can tell our riddles,
Not even the gods know its answers,
Nobody can trace our puzzles, not even
Magicians can place it right, I can tell
You the parable of the blind and you
Tell me the fables of the cripple.

The night has come, hold me tight
dear friend that I may not fall the fall
Of death, for I'm your sight to see the

Heart of the dusk, and you are my shanks to walk down the alley of darkness,

## The Street Legend

Do not mind the rag I wore,

Do not mind the scars on

my legs for barefooted I saunter,

The street stones have a record of my footprints, and they know I am famous and notorious.

Do not mind my filthy skin,

Do not mind my bushy hairs, for am not

A friend of any barber, I am called a street

Legend, for every nook and cranny I know, this street is my home for it made me famous.

All the paths in the bushes I know, for with my catapult I follow the Weaver bird, if not for the braveness and fierceness of the lion, the king of the forest I could have also become, am a legend in this street, for this is where I was born.

Do not worry who will beat the drum, just tell me if you are ready to dance, should I sing the songs of bones and marrow? or you want to dance to our traditional gongs and toros, you know I am multi-talented, that's why I am called a street legend.

I wish I was opportune to go to school, I would have told my teacher many tales, I would have told them why the leopard has many spots and why the tortoise walks so slow, I would have told them why the ants work so hard and why the grasshopper appears too lazy, I am the street legend because am notorious.

## Wrinkles Of Grace

These wrinkles are mine,

Life's worries in circles we dine,

For I have battled through the puzzles of time, my strength through these riddles is sublime, there are undefined crinkles around this lifeline, the wrinkles of grace.

These wrinkles are mine,

At this stage, they can never resign, for its design is divine, at this line I have coupled my punches, for this at my prime, I confine, through the rays of this race I found these wrinkles, the wrinkles of grace.

These wrinkles are mine,

Through the dewy eves and the noontide, these memories, in my veins at big times abide, to these feelings, I was never a slave or concubine, for I was found by a genuine ray, the rays of furrows of grace.

## The Familiar Foe In Winter

I know of a familiar foe in winter, this rival I know, a long time ago, who dresses in sheep's clothing

from head to toe, his smile glitters like a diamond in the cold, but his net is sure, it catches both young and old.

I know of this familiar foe, his creed, most agreed, in his vineyard, you must conceive, his Apostles embrace their creed,

to join this crew, your eyes must bleed, this urge they must feed uncountable times, even when their heart pleads.

I know of this familiar foe, his doctrine is so unkind to mankind,

In his handshake lies a bond to bind, at his feast, there are always friends and foes to dine, for he either makes you a slave or concubine.

I know of this familiar foe, so thin, but a king in his lane, he makes a giant heart either cripple or lame, in winter or summer new converts are welcomed in his name, and he aims to always become the king of the game.

I know of this familiar foe, he stands at the gate, ready to terminate, looking so handsome, his heart so sinful and grieved like inmates, to eat his meal, you need no plate, his name is " CIGARETTE".

## Bread Of Sorrow

We are children of the highest God, on the same ship sailing through the river Nile, of the same kind looking up to Jah, one bond has come to bind like clays on molded jars. upon this sea of horror we sail, for the bread of sorrow is here to serve.

On this journey we embark, prisoners of the same kind they took us, we are not convicts in this pool of crime, for out of the clay we were made, black souls who dispersed in search of greener pastures, but why has this come to be, for we never wished for this bread, the bread of sorrow.

Our flag we must raise, for if we ever lose sight of this shore at least our message we have passed, these storms of life made us

skilled sailors, for we never accepted this bread, the bread of sorrow.

Please do not shut these doors of struggles, do not worship the truth they told you in the day for at dawn the are bunch of lies, like

Candles in the wind. at least the world saw our sweats, they were the fuel that kept our candles

burning, for this bread they will bring to you, the bread of sorrow.

The night is near, I must go, for the captain of this ship I am, if we ever sailed to the east and never return, please remember to inscribe our names on the tablet of struggles, tell our children the battles we fought, tell them never

to relent, for these battles they must continue to fight if they ever wish to see the sunrise.

## Where We Belong

Home is where we belong,
in its nostrils, we feel among,
where tales of ancient tongues
were told at young, and melodies
of sweet lullabies abide with drums.

Home is where we belong,
in its walls, memories are drawn,
Where cuddle of infants songs began, for love like the mountain lilies cluster, and hunger like the fearless bees never stung,

Home is where we belong
where shadows of what we
will become lay with plum,
for contentment like no other
Whispers in crumbs.

Home is where we belong,
when our childhood was like movies untold, the tricks in Nollywood we never understood,
all was good, lyrics of hatred were never written for every nook and cranny we know until this tender hood became wild.

## In The Wings Of Time

There stands a golden time,

the time that awakens the link

of love, there stands a golden rule,

the rule that governs the bonds of love, there dangles a box of darling tales, which will illuminate the aisle of men, only in the

wings of time.

When the lazy souls of men have gone nigh to rest, there wanders a translucent bond, to glue the lonely selves that whimper, whisperings roar in this hour of the dusk, when the wakeful eyes of the mountain owl examine through the nostrils of the twilight for an intense prey that dares.

This is the only golden link, that never shrinks, for these elegant fantasies were told without a wink, let's paint this alley a colorful tender pink, with countless smiles and kisses without a blink, let's cuddle our memories with an infant sigh, for this is the bond that has vowed to bind our promises only in the wings of time.

Our nest we shall build like one clan, our wrongs we shall execute like heartless cain, our memories in these ageless walls shall hang like yams on a bountiful barn, for in this golden bond of love shall the wonders of the world be made visible to elucidate the hostile palate of our assailants.

## Medal Of Honor

This race I know is over,
the banquet of death I left over,
through the wings of time, I crossed over, my fears and terror from the nostrils of the dusk layover, and now I behold the glittering of these ribbons, the medal of honor.

Do not walk me down this alley of darkness, for my garment, I cannot find spotless, through these hills of grapple, my hope stood with boldness, like the brook toads my victory has woken the river goddess and has kept in bluntness the swords of the Invisibles.

Whistle not fear into the hearts of this night, for I wrestled this demon overnight, like sweet lullabies, this poem shall they recite, like tales of twilight its lyrics the shall rewrite, for I am the only knight with these
Medal and this fire of doom I have ignited.

Worry not, for grace found this warrior, my faith in shambles was never inferior, the tales of the lost lay in memorial their deeds at dawn were notorious, the lyrics of their songs remain victorious for the heart of these medals shall remain glorious.

## Beautiful Imperfections

Take me the way I am, for I am a being with adorable deformities, count not my sins, for my head is abundant with ugly memories.

Towards this evening tide, I and my imperfections sail through this river so slow like a predator, for like a mouse upon the monitor I wander without destination, please let go of my sins before this night grows old.

Hostility knocks on my door, but I am on a voyage to find who I will become, send me your love with beautiful roses for they alone can put smiles on my face again.

Paint not my deeds with crayon, for life has gifted us imperfections like Santa, let's enjoy this moment while we can, for like images on a broken mirror our guilt are convergent and divergent.

Like bread and butter, let's cuddle our errors, Like pestle and mortar we pound our past, for into this silent limbo of the past we cast our worries, into its wings we shall let go of our vices.

# Poems By Suchismita Ghoshal

## Eternity

To the unrequited love and the heartaches,

To the invincible feelings failed to get her some comfort,

To the sharp fabricated inconveniences from the unsympathetic being lying on opposite,

To the limerence aroused from a sacred birth of emotions,

And to the rose that bled deeply with her own thorns,

My wishes flow for your eternal events, etched on God's doors.

## Salvation

Dream-catchers helplessly curve their way towards my home,
Their crimson disguise gives birth to the intense passion I hide in,
The world seems to be an unapologetically genuine place
And all the theoretical distractions are embroidered on my Kurta!

## **Ages**

Ages have passed since she swimmed the river of emotions and reached the shore of ultimate pacification;

Ages have passed since her seraphic eyes drew the maps of her liberty.

## Love-Language

Synonym of poems is written in love language,
The language which picks the stories from heart to mind,
And beseeches abstracts to be adorned
On the very day of the language comprehension.

## Dreamlines

Senile skin was exfoliated,
Her voluptuous hair could entangle fairy tales in them,
She penetrated minds with her ecstatic tenderness
& life tucked the rainbow in her entity.

## Symmetry Of Love

Those reposeful eyes, ostentatious posture,
Bejeweled with the prominence of artist,
Blessed by the fascination of deities;
All of these consolidate on one point
From wooing my mind to your mind!

## Artistry

Artistry in my eyes,
My Kohl paints the desire of togetherness,
Unison is in my heart's hue,
Leaving me in the nostalgic ride of life.

## Nomadic Insanity

The vagabond mind roams
From one core to another for it seeks art only!
The calamities are a form of tumultuous synchrony of thoughts,
Art assassinates the waves within,
Taking her to find the divine ecstasy she has sought since ever!

## **Freedom**

Her aesthetic earrings could echo the emotions
of her suppressed heart,
She had a sanctuary of abstinence.
She could marry her freedom,
She procrastinates more to follow the path of divinity,
Her earrings being the beats of heart
Could resonate with the sacrifices she made for the journey ahead!

# Ice-Cream

Did I ever love the cities so much
That any stumble made me feel
The coldness can actually hold
The warmth of an ice-cream
And the shared talks would carry so much of death?

## Heritage

The heritage we used to dive in
Are getting glorification from the world now.
People transforming their outlook all of a sudden,
Rushes all around to own them through their sight of newly woke indulgence
Or is it re-discovering the faith they left behind?

## **Inheritance**

Stories will not end,
Generations will continue to blossom,
And minds will cut the puritanical aspects off for good.
Once in a while the city gets the junction to meet the old.
The old, the gigantic emblem of many histories stands up still.
Can tradition be forgotten with a swipe of modernism?

## Glorification

Teas and old alleys,
Witness humans more than anything.
The last days are submitted on a tarnished corner of our hearts
When kisses were whispering the lofiness of love,
The nobleness of caring for each other
On a warm cup of tea
Or, maybe the enigmatic pages of a novel
That would glorify them more often!

# Apocalypse

Beautified for innumerable times,
Lacks the encouragement coming from
The very layer of a self-surrendered soul.
Appreciated for endless bravery,
Miscomprehended for the over-embellishment
Mentioned by the rogues of extravagances!

## Traits Of A Bohemian

Bohemian soul,
Wanders here and there like a nomad,
Did it wish to be found back?
Did it wish to be loved back?
Unblemished art occurs,
It stirs with the colors of traditionals
To be desired back to the roads of iridescence!

## About the Authors

Nwankwo Chukwuma Levi

*Nwankwo Chukwuma Levi, popularly Known as "thefearlesspoet" is a Biafran poet, author, writer and editor, hails from* Mbaukwu, a town in Awka South L.G.A of Anambra state, Nigeria in the province of West Africa. Nwankwo wished to have his message passed across continents in black and white, his ink speaks both local and international languages as his pen was nicknamed "The mouthpiece of the gods of poetry" through a local poetry contest. Facts had it that through his birth poetry rose to the world, he is one of the magical writers who believe in the powers of their bleeding pen. He is one of the pen magicians in the world of poetry and other areas of literary creations. He has gotten many honors to his name through his magical writings. He won the poet of the week in "Pen is mightier", an international poetry platform, with the poem, "WRINKLES OF GRACE" winning the poet of the fourth night in "Avenue of poets". His poem "WHERE WE BELONG" won the poet of the week in "Pen is mightier" with the poem "SINNER'S CREED" won the poet of the week in "Passion of poetry". The list of his incredible poems goes on as his poem "HUNTER'S TALES" won the poet of the month in "Poetic warriors" as well as the poem "BARREN BEAUTY". He is the author of "HOW TO LOVE YOUR WIFE UNCONDITIONALLY", "SECRET OF SELF

IMPROVEMENT", "WRINKLES OF GRACE", "HEROES OF LIBERTY", "WHERE WE BELONG" and other creative works with their publication on AMAZON.COM. Nwankwo is currently based in Lagos Nigeria, West Africa

Contact Details:

+2347049826385

+2347044632292

Email address: Chimanwankwo1992 @gmail.com

NWANKWO CHUKWUMA LEVI
(Author, Writer, Poet & Editor)
BIAFRA, WEST AFRICA
BOOKS:
"WRINKLES OF GRACE"
"HEROES OF LIBERTY"
"SECRET OF SELF IMPROVEMENT"
"HOW TO LOVE YOUR WIFE UNCONDITIONALLY"
All on Amazon.com.
EMAIL: chimanwankwo1992@gmail.com

**Suchismita Ghoshal**

*Author Suchismita Ghoshal hails from West Bengal, India. At the age of 25, she has been continuously leaving her footprints in the contemporary literary world. She is a widely published author, internationally reputed bilingual poet, spoken word poet, professional writer, content writer, editor and critic, language translator, interpreter and transcriptor (Bengali, English), performing poet, communicator and literary influencer, an independent thinker, humanitarian, change enthusiast and philanthropist. She's been invited to many international festivals and open mics. Her awards, accolades and achievements not only inspire her more to write but also to influence her through the kindness of her words. Her solo books "Fields of Sonnet", "Emotions & Tantrums" & "Poetries in Quarantine" are available on Amazon website. She collaborated with the famous Greek children's author, Miss Eva Petropoulou Lianoy for her impeccably conceptualized fourth literary book, "An Ecstatic Renaissance Between Greece and India Through Poetry" by the efficiency of internationally reputed traditional publication farm, Ukiyoto Publishing House. She strives towards all the good things and keeps her high-spirits up for miracles to happen.*

**SUCHISMITA GHOSHAL**
(Author, Writer, Poet, Editor & Influencer)
West Bengal India.
BOOKS:
"Fields of Sonnet"
"Emotions & Tantrums"
Poetries in Quarantine"
"An Ecstatic Renaissance Between Greece & India Through Poetry"
(All on Amazon.com)
Email: creativesuchismista2909@gmail.com

www.ingramcontent.com/pod-product-compliance
Lightning Source LLC
LaVergne TN
LVHW041558070526
838199LV00046B/2043